Clothes Poems

Compiled by John Foster

Contents

Acknowledgements

The Editor and Publisher wish to thank the following who have kindly given permission for the use of copyright material:

Ann Bonner for 'Dirty dress' © 1991 Ann Bonner; Marie Brookes for 'The lost sock' © 1991 Marie Brookes; John Coldwell for 'My clean blouse' © 1991 John Coldwell; John Foster for 'Shoes' and 'There's a hole in my pants' both © 1991 John Foster; Judith Nicholls for 'Welly-walk' © 1991 Judith Nicholls; Irene Yates for 'Princess Kirandip' © 1991 Irene Yates.

The lost sock

I've lost one of my socks.
It's yellow and blue.
Now I've only one sock.
This morning I'd two.

I've lost one of my socks.
I've looked everywhere.
This morning I'd two—
And two make a pair.

2

I've lost one of my socks.
What shall I do?
How did it get there?
It's inside my shoe!

Marie Brookes

Shoes

Red shoes, blue shoes,
Old shoes, new shoes,
Shoes that are black,
Shoes that are white,
Shoes that are loose,
Shoes that are tight.
Shoes with buckles,
Shoes with bows,
Shoes that are narrow
And pinch your toes.

Shoes that are yellow,
Shoes that are green,
Shoes that are dirty,
Shoes that are clean.
Shoes for cold weather,
Shoes for when it's hot.
Shoes with laces
That get tangled in a knot!

John Foster

There's a hole in my pants

There's a hole in my pants.
It's our washing machine.
It's eating our clothes,
Not washing them clean.

As it churns round and round,
It snorts and it snickers,
Chewing holes in Dad's shirts
And ripping Mum's knickers.

It's swallowed a sock.
We can't open the door.
It's bubbling out soap suds
All over the floor.

There's a monster that lives
In our washing machine.
It's eating our clothes,
Not washing them clean.

John Foster

7

Princess Kirandip

At school in the week
I wear
A grey skirt and
Green jumper, just like my best friend
And we pretend we're twins.
But on Saturdays and Sundays
I wear my
Shiny, shiny blue
Kameeze and langa
With a tuni to cover my head,
All covered with silver stars—
And Tracey
Stares at me and says
'Oh, Kirandip—
You must be a princess!'

And I feel good.

Irene Yates

My clean blouse

Look at my blouse!
It was clean today.
I tried very hard
To keep it that way.

Do you like my painting?
It's a bird in the sky.
But I leaned on the paper
Before it was dry.

Then at play time I joined in
A great game of chase
But I tripped on a stone
And fell flat on my face.

At lunch time, somebody,
Peter, I think,
Bumped into me just as I
Picked up my drink.

Then on the way home
I was splashed by a lorry.
I tried to stay clean, Mum.
Believe me. I'm sorry.

John Coldwell

14

Dirty dress

Egg-yolk yellow.
Lollipop pink.
Red tomato ketchup.
Spilt orange drink.

Brown mud and gravy.
What a mess!
All the day's colours
On my baby sister's dress.

Ann Bonner

Welly-walk

Squelching in the oak leaves,
splashing in the sea;
sploshing in the puddles,
dry as dry can be.

Kicking, tripping, sliding,
sinking in the mud;
crunching, marching, gliding
down the snowy road.

Judith Nicholls